That Lone Ship

That Lone Ship

Rhys Owain Williams

PARTHIAN

Parthian, Cardigan SA43 1ED www.parthianbooks.com
First published in 2018
© Rhys Owain Williams 2018
ISBN 978-1-912109-24-1
Editor: Susie Wild
Cover design by Torben Schacht
Typeset by Alison Evans
Printed in EU by Pulsio SARL
Published with the financial support of the Welsh Books Council
British Library Cataloguing in Publication Data
A cataloguing record for this book is available from the British Library.

For my mother

Contents

Haiku	1
En Dash	3
A New Year	4
Ghazal	5
Waiting Room	6
The Pint that Follows	7
Bonaparte Before the Sphinx	8
Eglwyswrw	10
Drowned	11
Haiku	13
Gull	14
The First Time	16
School Eisteddfod	17
Reunion Tour	18
Victoria Park, 5 a.m.	19
Haiku	21
The Man at the Bus Stop	22
The Road Must Eventually Lead to the Whole World	24
The M4	25
We Weren't Interested in Girls	28
Gastrophthalmophobia	29
Bookshop Evacuation at the Edinburgh Festival	30
Haiku	33
Excavation	34
Geosmin	35
The Walk to Work	36
Polaroid	39
They Sang *Gwahoddiad*	40
Haiku	43
A Minute's Silence	44
New Shirt	45
Vetch Field Elegy	46

58 Years   48
The Search Party   49
Third Boy (Dicky)   50
Marking Out the Ground with String   52
The End   53

Notes on the Poems   55
Acknowledgements   57

that lone ship on the horizon
   arriving or leaving?

En Dash

We begin – our souls as thin
as silverskin onions,
caught breathless in the danger
that follows the fourth digit.

Then, loaded by that first gulp of air,
we sink our hook into its side,
scramble up, join others
in
        squinting –

Years pass, we learn to forget
that the en dash will ever end.
We dance hard, test the strength
of its span, lose track of time.
We are all so alive, so far
from
        falling –

You say you have found a lump.
The appointment is next Tuesday.
It will be okay, you say, you're sure
that it's
        nothing –

A New Year

The years are storm-straddled,
crag-black hooves thundering between headlands,
kicking up hailstones,
washing sandbagged towns to the sea.
But, this afternoon, jaws clamp open,
and all surface water reflects a fresh blue page.

So go outside, and with the winter sun on your neck,
a crisp shock of air in your lungs, tune out
the fore-echo of hoofbeats, the sound
of the storm about-turning. A new year stretches out
as empty as mirrors, though no doubt still heavy
with the weight of a first bite.

Ghazal

Outside the front door of a mid-terrace house
wedding photos spill from a split black bag.

In summer, we enjoy a barbecue on the beach
but the sausages dropped on the sand go uneaten.

The next day, despite the hours between us,
my fingers still cling to your faint perfume.

Although I find her number in a charity shop shirt,
I do not phone to see if she was unwanted too.

Despite what Hollywood would have you think,
nobody makes love in slow motion.

Morning – a dried slug curled up on the carpet
brought through the house with last night's bins.

To feel the sting of aftershave on his freshly-cut jaw,
the felled soldier would kill many, many times more.

Waiting Room

9.45
lies the white
plastic clock

stopped

just as you had.
We chased across
town, chancing

down one-ways
to sit

      waiting

drinking

unnecessary tea.
Then, the only news
my itchy eyes

could take.
They had you
ticking again.

The Pint that Follows

Story unloaded and beer sunk, he asks me: *Do you think I've done the right thing?* [Pause]. *Yes,* I say, but not because it's what he wants to hear. Because it's true. There really is no point in being unhappy.

We sit for a few minutes in comfortable silence. *There are difficult weeks ahead*, I say, *but you'll get through them. And then there'll be something else, something new, and you'll feel better.* He smiles, half-believing me. I cringe at how rehearsed my response sounds, as if I've lifted it from a film.

> frothy dregs drained,
> a glass
> ready to be refilled

We'll be here again, having this pint. Maybe I'll be the one with the reddened eyes and sleep-starved skin. Maybe it'll be him. But no matter which one of us it is, the other will be here. Buying the pints. Lending his ears.

Bonaparte Before the Sphinx

'In the first half of the nineteenth century, Swansea was copper smelter not just to Britain, but to the world.'
– Ronald Rees, *King Copper*

This hard winter mud
commits shoe prints,
faint notches on a footpath
not yet ready for school trips.

There are statues here now,
      the smelters remembered.

Tip of my nose warmed
by underbite breath,
                I pause.
Their tales of ore reforged
by speakerbox voices.
Words rise above smoke stacks,
fertilise
           scorched ground.

Don't you remember
when this town was important?
When salted barques carved copper lodes
beyond the bounded Severn Sea.

Upstream, we have ripped up
the monkey puzzle's roots,
swept the dust of industry into
Wetherspoons picture frames,
built a concrete river
using leftover slag.

Here, backhoes are working the old bones
like larder beetles,
this copperworks carcass
                picked clean.
Ready
      to mount.

Though summer will bring crowds,
ice-cream chimes,
                unfolding tinfoil,
for now, there's just a lone figure,
fresh tarmac.
The heavy silence of monoliths.

Eglwyswrw

The cracked ribs of umbrellas
pierce sopping black bags.
For three months it has rained.
Clogged drains making rivers
of cobbled inclines, testing
the patience of bitumen, creating
a village of soft boot soles.

Now, the sun hits this
tissue-plugged sink,
a hand dryer to a sweat patch.
It edges the blur,
returns sharp borders.
And back on the hook,
the newspaper man's room key.

*** * * *

On the Mount, the old man
had matched up the animals,
disassembled his cowshed.
As the sun falls too quickly
he catches the last of it,
peaked shadows dancing
below a sheet-metal pyre.

Drowned

I dreamt that you had drowned.
Your clothed body caught in the reeds
                of a silent river,
so far upstream that the canopy hung
thick as cobwebs.

Breaking my own rule, I wake and tell
how they left you there:
                a pale white warning
of currents too fast.
Not bloated by water, but
        thin
              sleeping
                      preserved
  (though maybe turtles had begun
to snap beneath the surface).

  You say I'm the last to visit – a day's
trek through the scrub to sit with your
ghost.
                We skirt the eroteme,
              make offal of tongue,
until, eventually, you sliver the hush:

        It was her dress, you say,
enveloping, unstringing,
              her and her dress
        coiling around us like rope,
            dragging us under.

Morriston Cross – the parting of ways
where I should have kissed her

a break in clouds –
the sea, no longer grey
but nuclear yellow

midnight stride
through the underpass –
haunted by leaves

snow-prints –
in the wake of man's shoe,
a paw

Gull

'Why we have so many gulls in poetry these days is a matter for reflection.'

– Peter Sansom, *Writing Poems*

I

On a wrinkled edge of rooftop cliff,
you might catch a lull,
see a flash of beauty in my withdrawal,
find comfort in shared silence.
But lose me to the frenzy of flapping wings
and our link is severed.
I am just like the others.
See the ripple of long-dead monsters
in my gait,
and in my eyes the slow attend
of monsters still to come.

II

August is the kindest month, discarded
chip paper from ungrateful hands, mixing
vinegar and ice cream, stirring
wings, a glutton's screech.

Replenish this dinner plate.

Cover these streets in what you cannot eat,
keep us sweet
with cold sausage rolls,
crumbs from crisp packets.
An empty belly is a sharpened beak,
a talon-scrape across tender hands.

III

At low tide, see the squabble die.
Dusk brings with it an uneasy peace.
The well-oiled shock of this machine
reduced, now, to watching, waiting.
Yes, predators come to take our young,
the search for higher ground breeds tension,
but above the mew and choke we rise as one.
It is not impossible
to see us soar.

The First Time

You say you don't remember the first time.
It was your birthday, on the kitchen counter

an empty bottle of black sambuca. Drinking
first, then drank, then drunk you kissed me

in the bathroom mirror, mouthed *let go, let's
go to bed*. Curtain corners held back the dawn,

the house asleep, and above the covers our
bodies clung, caught together. Alarm bells rang,

you slipped away, your thin black dress eluding
fingertips, our waking friends. *Not yet*, you said,

not yet. Though the next afternoon, your hand
found mine, when no one was looking.

School Eisteddfod

For 'Sospan Fach'
I sang too fast
he says
placing me joint-third
one from last
although
only four of us competed.

Reunion Tour

This is what time travel must feel like.

Light between the cracks
in our dusted-down leathers,
the crowd a wave of weakening crowns.
Here is the return
               of fish net, blue streaks,
the smell of soapbar hash and pit sweat.
The band take the stage,
a reverb of pubescence
               but the singer's tired
and they've replaced the bassist.
This re-echo isn't what I remember.

Then that chorus hits.

Back in that bedroom, I sink below
a floor-wardrobe bulwark,
a resting Gulliver before a jewel-case sea.
Soon, islanders will come
with their pegs and string,
               measure me up
for a life among lookalikes.
Door shut to that world, I build
a palisade with rolled-up posters,
call upon a battalion
               of Blu-Tacked gods.

And in these seconds
counted by strobes,
the last bars shaving the years thin,
hope there will be time
               for one more song.

Victoria Park, 5 a.m.

Curtains remain closed
to this morning's morning,
as gaps between houses
play host
to the sun's hide-and-seek.
                        Sodden,
I tilt into gardens,
beheading biennials.
Your makeshift bouquet.

We were breaching ground then,
though still unsaid.
                    Ready to root,
but not share the same bed.

Advance quickened
by faces misplaced
in pale Guildhall windows.
The complaints of orange-
peeled gates do not deter,
beneath the flaky white tears
of Adelina
                    I de-flower.

Then, walking back over
empty parking spaces,
through the photograph
of my graduating father,
I wonder what will follow
from this uncertain moment:

the first light
    that even birds sleep through.

abandoned churchyard –
cairns of broken headstones
shaded by alder leaves

                                      pinched from the plughole,
                                    a kinked strand of red hair
                                          catches last light

helicopter buzz
draws us to front doors,
birds land on rooftops

                                              urban autumn –
                                      coloured leaves caught
                                        in takeaway cartons

The Man at the Bus Stop

We collect,
sheltered by two-thirds of a box,
                              gathered in hope
                                  of the 8.42

He is there without fail.
            His eyes rubber-stalking the bend.
Muttering half-questions.
                      We pretend not to hear.

'There's something wrong with him,'
                            they say
                in a pensioner's whisper,
                      'He's not all there.'

At the first sliver of painted steel
his arms fly up,
                'I'M HERE!
                          I'M HERE!'
Louder than the halt
                of route-weary wheels.
                          I'm here.

***

It is night now, the buses have stopped.
I pause too long in the room
where our toothbrushes touch.
Through the open window,
the silent world
           leans,
                and I say
                      nothing.

The Road Must Eventually Lead to the Whole World

We told friends we'd drive the whole coast of Britain, but we only got as far as Penzance. As we left Swansea on that lukewarm morning, I had a feeling we wouldn't make it past Cornwall. Petrol prices had skyrocketed that year. When we reached Mount's Bay, we sat in the car in a car park, unwilling to pay and display. It was Saturday, and day-tripping tourists had taken over the town. We both agreed it was time to head home – back to part-time jobs, our comfortable beds. Three days on the road and our hometown was calling us – its high, clear song carried on the haze. *Bring your ship to rest so that you may hear our voices.* That night, we pitched on a hill on Devon's north coast, trying to cook tinfoil-wrapped sausages under the hood of my car. Across the Severn Sea, I was sure I could see Mumbles Lighthouse, shining a light through the unsighted night.

The M4

clinging to my wing mirror,
the spider
and her now-mobile home

---

the church tower, yes,
from my car on the motorway,
but not the crows

---

like acupuncture needles,
twenty wind turbines
pinprick the hilltop

---

strung to the bridge:
a bouquet of flowers,
lifeless in the wind

🛣

washed clean by the rain,
an advertisement board
with nothing to sell

🛣

across the toll bridge,
a lone seagull follows
the course of my car

🛣

searching for earthworms
on a field of picked corn,
the jackdaws dance

🛣

a red triangle cenotaph
at the woodland's edge
'deer crossing'

🛣

heavy foot on brake pedal,
the car slows
to sprint-runner speed

🛣

a broken engine
on a rag and bone pick-up
makes one last journey

🛣

motorway footbridge
a man and child
pause
watch others speed by

We Weren't Interested in Girls

We just wanted to play football. While the rest of the boys in our year were out shagging (or at least claiming to be), we were on the hunt for makeshift goal posts. The bins round the back of the school. Two saplings planted up in the park. The garage doors at the top of Tirpenry Street. Jumpers didn't cut it. Sometimes we'd break into the Astroturf, though security guards soon put a stop to that. Every night without fail, the five of us would be outside with a ball, scoring goals and making saves. Then, one summer, I went off with her. Soon after, they all got girlfriends too. We'd still meet up and play football sometimes, but it wasn't the same. We'd let our defences down, and adulthood had crept in at the back post.

Gastrophthalmophobia

noun.
   1. the fear of being stared at whilst eating

In the window of the café
near the Kingsway traffic lights
an insecure sandwich-eater
waits on green for his next bite.

Bookshop Evacuation at the Edinburgh Festival

Standing at *Poetry and Plays*,
I hear Velcro
        c r e p i t a t e
                    as loop is betrayed
                        by cohort hook.

The couple next to me
                (browsing *Classics*)
point at the portion of sky
that has entered the bookshop
                      uninvited.

Realisation sweeps
across the carpeted floor:
the tent is collapsing.

Few take a moment to discuss the

        unfolding

                    situation.
Most go back to books,
        reading blurbs,
                judging covers,
                      quite unfazed
by the disaster
        that heads towards us from above.

        HUNDREDS BURIED AS
        BOOK TENT COLLAPSES

reads the headline of *The Times*.

Whereas *The Sun* merrily runs
with

        BOOKWORMS PULPED!

Our literary grazing interrupted
by a bullhorn-equipped altruist.
    'Can you vacate the tent please?'
                  he asks,
    before retracting his question mark,
        escorting us to the exit.

Un-bought books are prised out of hands,
returned to shelves by cashiers
who perform
        Indiana
           Jones
              rolls,
                  escaping
            just before canvas
                meets carpet.

        ***

In the resulting melee,
a purple-rinsed pensioner totters off.
Taking an unplanned turn to a life of
crime,
she leaves without paying
    for a discounted Burns anthology
        and two Ian Rankins.

smothered in cream,
she does not see the plum I gave her
was bruised

                                    cool summer shade –
                                            three boys
                                    with bare wrists

view from Townhill:
my house, the city –
much smaller than the sea

                                  found beneath floorboards,
                                  three un-paired shoes
                                  break death's silence

Excavation

Browned elastic bands, close to snapping,
grip the inscriptions on used tickets, expired

coupons, a faded proof of buried treasure.
Artefacts unstacked, your palms become

soup spoons – blunt pencils, spent batteries,
a locked lock without a key. Then the dislodge

of a stamped passport, a love note written in
unbroken hand. This quiet box a portal now,

an unsettling of prehistory. See how the world
turned without your weight, and how it circles

still – to make hollow by removing the inner part
can leave more than just a hole to fill.

Geosmin

Taken
in a sea of hands
from an unbuttoned pocket:
the camera that captured
               then held
our frames of light.
The thief's stomach now full,
their elbow crook bruised.

           ***

Across the center of the world
we'd paused,
        caught between pulses,
feigned the stilling of time.

Now returned to unlaundered sheets,
we cling to half-remembered panoramas.
Talk about the busker in Washington Square.
Share our cloudy mental pictures.
The only proof.

           ***

      You, near the lake,
      unedited;
      the undersong of leaves,
      the smell
                of

The Walk to Work

'I am constantly waiting for something to kick in.'
– graffiti found in Uplands, Swansea

At the head of Bryn-y-Mor, an old man with a sandwich board waves at morning commuters. *Jesus Loves You. Mae Iesu'n Caru Ti.* Though the air is heavy with the possibility of snow, white daffodils have begun to sprout in the flowerbeds of St James's churchyard. Bus-stop acquaintances discuss the price of petrol.

> tight to the lamp post –
> a crowd of white stargazers,
> envelope still sealed

Twenty minutes from opening, a barber sweeps the last of yesterday's hair from his floor. Breaching the nimbostratus, sunlight bounces between his polished chrome, springing out of the shop's front door to blind the street's eyes and windows. Exhaust fumes rise from the line of traffic on Walter Road, mixing with the smell of coffee beans and microwaved bacon.

Two boys in hoods pass me, pushing cement mixers like prams. For some, the working day's countdown has already begun. Outside the English language centre, a circle of well-wrapped men speak in a more comfortable tongue.

> cracking old tarmac
> on the tree-cleared boulevard –
> the memories of roots

Over Mansel Street, three bras hang in solidarity, supported by the raised wire that runs between Bunnies Health Club and the Women's Aid. Anti-climb fence panels surround the old Albert Hall's crumbling edges. The street is being spot-cleaned, renovated in patches. In the centre of a freshly-painted white wall, a black marker-pen message: *Wendy I still love you.*

> caught on my sleeve,
> a long, flickering strand
> of someone else's hair

Trigger-happy snoozers, running too late to break the fast at home, dive in and out of Tesco Extra – promising themselves that tomorrow morning will bring porridge, a slow cup of tea. Three half-drunk lager bottles sit abandoned outside the magistrates' court. Half-full, or half-empty? Changing traffic lights at the crossroads force a switch to the pavement on the other side. Must keep moving forward.

> at Clifton Hill's foot,
> a runaway orange wrinkles
> in the winter sun

A shortcut takes the route past the Ragged School. *Fovnded 1847. Rebvilt 1911.* A free education for the children of the Victorian slums. Later a soup kitchen, a bomb shelter. Now, in these gentler times, Swansea's *Centre for Psychic & Educational Healing.* Amongst the notices Blu-Tacked to its window: ingredients for a recipe from the Dyfatty Street food bank, and a flyer advertising a coach trip to the jungle of Calais.

> bolt without thunder –
> from a loose flagstone,
> a shot of old rainwater

From the train station pour the straphangers – suited and booted for careers in indifference. They stream out of Ivey Place, down High Street, across Alexandra Road. Pavement maintenance creates a bottleneck outside The Grand Hotel, giving sleepy Swansea a taste of Waterloo and Victoria, Liverpool Street and King's Cross. As the minutes tick towards 9 o'clock, the remaining crowd withdraws to buses, taxis, shops, cafés. At the station's entrance, a busker strums beneath Pete Ham's blue plaque. The familiar lyrics rise into the air, making their way as far as the open window on Alexandra House's fourth floor.

> clouds gather –
> an old man empties a bag of rock salt
> that looks like snow

Polaroid

On that Saturday after the snow
we took instant pictures
on the beach before bedtime,
squinting into the darkness
of the developing snaps,
trying to make out faces
before they were there.

In the adventure playground
you sat on a bench,
wearing my coat

FLASH!

You hated it.
Wanted to rip it up
under the street light.

I wouldn't let you.

I want to keep it
for when we have both faded,
gathered dust and grown old,
for a time when my hand
may no longer find yours.
I want to keep
········you,
wearing my coat,
on that Saturday after the snow.

They Sang *Gwahoddiad*

From a hospital bed,
you cancelled your subscription
to the daily news
peacefully
after a long illness
patiently borne.

We finally lost you
to tobacco smoke and chalk dust.

At your funeral, they sang *Gwahoddiad*;
the voices of Morriston
                          so loud
I'm sure you'd have heard them.

And I cried –
still the boy who had wished his Bamps
could come outside to play
instead of being stuck indoors,
short of breath.

From behind glass, you wished that too.

That boy heard you,
lungs *hwyl*-filled,
singing in the rows behind him:

Arglwydd, dyma fi
ar dy alwad di,
canna f'enaid
yn y gwaed
a gaed ar Galfari.

But dolour blurred the vision
of the black-tied man who'd grown.

Even the most sonorous of voices
cannot sing
         through
                 such

                       silence.

the morning so young,
bed sheets dry in the rain

                                perched on telephone wire,
                                      a lone crow caws
                                across the silent field

sharing a grave;
two strangers
    (her husbands)
waiting for her

                                    pulsing behind glass,
                                    the house cat catches
                             a glimpse of young magpies

A Minute's Silence

Across the ground, a pause
as still as the years that follow.

Matchday chat falls to the pit where
lost apple pips lie – feel them

stretch into this emptiness, burst into
boughs, touch all sides

of this amphitheatre struck dumb.
A crowded silence can seem so

deathless. Watch the whistle rise,
embrace the explosion.

New Shirt

She gave me a shirt
one of yours
though never worn
an unnecessary Christmas present
still boxed
sleeves safety-pinned
to the collar

so I un-box
un-pin
put it on
and
for the briefest
of moments

think of you

even though
you never wore it

and never will.

Vetch Field Elegy

*Swansea City vs. Wrexham, FAW Premier Cup Final,
Swansea, Wales, 11th May 2005*

On your deathbed
we stripped you.
Ripped out red plastic seats
and advertisement boards
like thieves
stealing gold from fresh bodies.

The Vetch clock,
not yet stopped
but definitely slowing,
tick-tocked our
final minutes away
as Roger Evans,
muffled by soot,
whispered down chimneys
into Sandfields living-rooms
for the last time.

Then, with makeshift spades
we dug shallow graves
across your boot-worn pitch.
Taking turf home
to place on the mantel,
to plant in back-gardens,

to say we were there
when that man in black
sounded the final final-whistle
at our beloved tin shed.

And as the smell
of warm piss and fried onions
drifted above the floodlights,
getting lost on its way to the bay,
we poured out into the streets
like black and white tears.

58 Years

*Gareth Bale, Wales vs. Slovakia, Euro 2016 Group B,
Bordeaux, France, 11th June 2016*

He's hit free kicks before.
Lifted them over memories
of spurned chances,
missed penalties.
Bent them round the shadows
of an unjust sporting past:
an East German and his missing flag,
a toothless Scot's veiled fist.
Some nestled in side-netting,
while others found a postage stamp.
Each one sent home dulls the thwack
of Bodin and his crossbar.

This one soars.
Not just above a Slovak wall,
six men wide, but beyond
the *Nouveau Stade*,
the French countryside.
Across the Severn Sea to land
in living rooms
and pubs and clubs,
to break a stretching absence heard
through fifty-eight tormented years.
As Kozáčik empties his net,
a nation cheers, for this reset.

The Search Party

A green Peugeot drives past us at Lake Bled. It's the same car we left outside our house in Swansea. We joke our cats are driving it, that they've followed us to Slovenia. *Hey jerks! Why did you leave us all alone in that big cold house?* Later, at Bled Castle, a German tourist takes our photograph while we eat our evening meal. He says he just wants the view behind us, but we know the truth. He's a private investigator, hired by the cats. *See what they're getting up to without us*, they tell him, *we'll make it worth your while.* Back home my mother is frantic, but she knows not to spoil a holiday with news of missing pets. She keeps a vigil on our back step, shakes the Go-Cat box for hours. The next day on Vršič Pass, we give another green Peugeot the slip. This time I clock the driver, a blonde woman wearing sunglasses. Our cats may be tailing us through Europe, but they still don't have opposable thumbs. This woman is their patsy, another victim of their manipulative feline ways. That night, I lie awake in Ljubljana, think of them existing unseen over a thousand miles away. I wonder if they know we'll return. I wonder if they care that we've gone.

Third Boy (Dicky)

'... he'll never forget as he paddles blind home
through the weeping end of the world.'
        – Dylan Thomas, *Under Milk Wood*

Each night,
on the darkened stage
behind my moon-burnt eyelids
I re-live it:

standing wet on the cobbles
in my patched-up pants
as the shrill girls giggle
and gaggle around me,
asking for kisses or pennies
to buy treats from Cockle Street
sweet-shop.

And I, refusing.

And always refusing.

Because my mother said
I mustn't kiss girls:
they torment and torture
young boys like me
– but really
because Tad couldn't keep
his grubby fingers from the jars
of the wild hovel women
who live upon the hills.

And so, 'neath the wood,
I refused to smack lips
with the village bike
(as she became known)
and ran
wee
wee
wee
all the way home
like a porking pig
squealing for his mother's pink teat.

And you ask how it makes me feel?

It makes me feel
as bitter as citrus skin,
as abandoned as bagged cats,
but as awakened as I will ever be,
understanding that the almighty omniscient
could have written a different part
for poor Dicky,
but didn't.

Marking Out the Ground with String

This is where their beds will be – can you see?
Side by side and perfectly symmetrical. Yes, one
may have a better view of the disappearing sun,
but the other has the lamplight. They will learn to share.

This rectangle here is where their books will go.
It may look small, but the stacked pages will reach
all the way to the ceiling. Only one of them will inherit
my fear of heights. We will buy them a ladder.

This square is the chest where their clothes will be kept,
uniforms ironed and folded during a Sunday night film.
One afternoon, the chest's weight will be pushed to the door,
keeping us out. Things will rarely be easy.

This circle is the chair, with its balding arms and
defeated springs. Within this nook we'll take turns to sit,
straining to hear the night's silence, watching them grow
by the hour. We must remember each other.

The End

At the end of the world,
those in cinema seats
remained set
until the credits rolled,
becoming the last to know
that history was about to reach
conclusion.

On the streets, families
raced to reach a last
clinch, a last glimpse
of the people they had
built their lives upon.
The pubs remained wet, as
shop shutters shut across
the high streets of the world,
their tills packed full of
paper less valuable
than those moments before
nothing.

And I dreamt that we would meet
on one of our city's seven hills,
hold hands as those below
dusted off their safety cards,
but you got caught in traffic,
and I couldn't outrun the reel.

Notes on the Poems

En Dash – An 'en dash' is a punctuation mark (–). One of its common uses is to indicate a span between two dates (e.g. the dates of a person's birth and death).

Ghazal – This poem is a loose, Westernised version of a 'ghazal' – an ancient form originating in 6th century arabic verse. Roughly pronounced like the English word 'guzzle', a ghazal is composed of five or more couplets that are thematically and emotionally autonomous.

Bonaparte Before the Sphinx – This poem takes its title from the 1886 painting by Jean-Léon Gérôme. Its epigraph is from page 1 of Ronald Rees's *King Copper: South Wales and the Copper Trade 1584-1895* (University of Wales Press, 2000).

Eglwyswrw – Eglwyswrw is a village in Pembrokeshire, Wales, where it rained for eighty-five consecutive days between October 2015 and January 2016. The village was five days short of beating the British record of eighty-nine days, set on the Scottish island of Islay in 1923.

Gull – This poem's epigraph is from pages 36–37 of Peter Sansom's *Writing Poems* (Bloodaxe Books, 1994).

Victoria Park, 5 a.m. – In 1918, opera singer Adelina Patti donated the winter garden pavilion from her Craig-y-Nos estate to the people of Swansea. It was reconstructed in the then-town's Victoria Park in 1920. Swansea's Guildhall (adjacent to Victoria Park) is the venue commonly used for the graduation ceremonies of the city's two universities.

The Road Must Eventually Lead to the Whole World – This poem takes its title from a line in Jack Kerouac's *On the Road* (Viking Press, 1957). 'Bring your ship to rest, so that you may hear our voices' is from E. V. Rieu's translation of Homer's *The Odyssey* (Penguin Classics, 1946). The line forms part of the song the Sirens sing to Odysseus, in the hope that they will lure him to shipwreck on their rocky coast.

Geosmin – 'Geosmin' is an organic compound with a distinct earthy aroma – a contributor to the strong scent that occurs in the air when rain falls after a prolonged spell of dry weather. 'The center of the world' is one of the many nicknames for New York City.

58 Years – Fifty-eight years is the length of time between the Wales men's national football team qualifying for the World Cup in 1958 and then reaching another major international tournament in 2016. In the time between, Welsh football fans were treated to a seemingly constant cycle of crushing lows and false dawns. The first stanza of this poem includes references to matches in 1976, 1977 and 1993, where Wales were painfully close to breaking their qualifying hoodoo. I am grateful for detailed accounts of these matches in Phil Stead's excellent *Red Dragons: The Story of Welsh Football* (Y Lolfa, 2012).

Third Boy (Dicky) – This poem is named after a minor character in Dylan Thomas's radio drama *Under Milk Wood* (1954). I am grateful to Weidenfeld & Nicolson and The Trustees for the Copyrights of Dylan Thomas for their permission to reprint an extract from *Under Milk Wood* as the poem's epigraph.

Acknowledgements

Acknowledgements are due to the editors of the following publications, in which some of these poems first appeared: *Agenda*; *Another Country: Haiku Poetry from Wales* (Gomer); *Blood and Thunder, Rough and Tumble: The Sandfields Story* (Sandfields Community Association); *bottle rockets*; *Graffiti*; *The Gull*; *The Haiku Calendar 2016* (Snapshot Press); *The Lampeter Review*; *Popshot*, *Square*; *Wales Haiku Journal*.

Some of the haiku in this collection were first seen as part of a permanent public art project at Morriston Hospital, Swansea. Thanks are due to the curators of that project: Art in Site and Abertawe Bro Morgannwg University Health Board. 'The First Time' was featured in the poetry showcase 'Let Go, Let's Go' as part of *New Welsh Review*'s multimedia programme. Readings of 'The End', 'Third Boy (Dicky)' and 'Vetch Field Elegy' were filmed for *The Crunch* Issue #0.

The road towards a first poetry collection is long and winding. A huge thank you to the following people for their advice, support and encouragement along the way: Adam Sillman, Richard James Jones, Emily Vanderploeg, Fflur Dafydd, Stevie Davies, Rhian Elizabeth, Jo Furber, Natalie Ann Holborow, David Hughes, Alan Kellermann, Rebecca Parfitt, Liza Penn-Thomas, clare e. potter, and all my fellow Hay Festival Writers at Work. Thank you to my editor Susie Wild – your thoughtful suggestions have improved this collection. A special mention goes to the late Nigel Jenkins, a sorely missed friend and mentor who taught me so much.

This collection would not have been possible without the support of my family and friends – love and thanks to you all. This book is dedicated to my mother, who I can safely say is (and has always been) my biggest fan.

Finally, to Laura. Thank you for reading every single draft I've ever handed you, for being willing to tell me what you don't like about a poem, for building me up on the bad days and keeping me grounded on the good ones. I couldn't do any of this without you.

Discover new writing with Parthian

THE LAST POLAR BEAR ON EARTH
RHIAN ELIZABETH

THAT LONE SHIP
RHYS OWAIN WILLIAMS

SALACIA
MARI ELLIS DUNNING

THE WAY OUT
KATE NORTH

www.parthianbooks.com